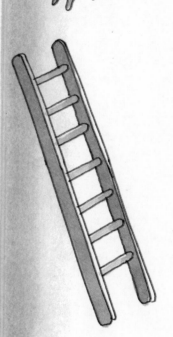

CONTENTS

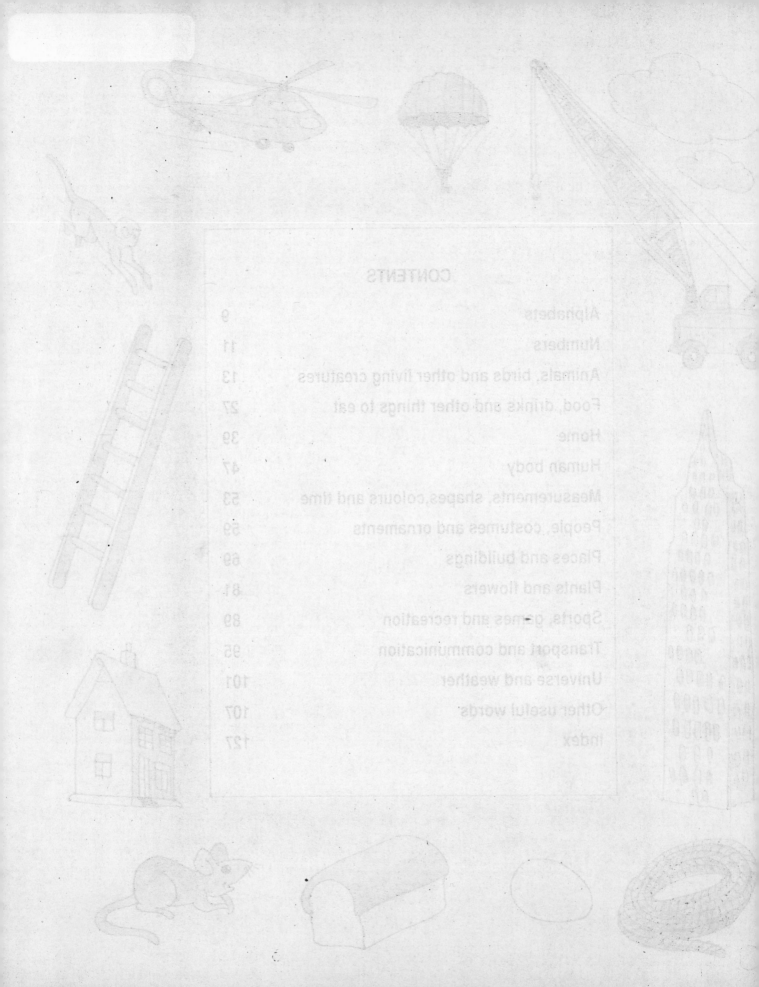

CONTENTS

ENGLISH – CHINESE

英漢

Editor
BABITA VERMA

designed by
MRINAL MITRA

STAR

CHILDREN'S PICTURE DICTIONARY

BILINGUAL

WITH
OVER 1,000 ENGLISH WORDS
CLASSIFIED IN
14 TOPICS

coordinating Artists :
**Soumitro Sarkar, Ramendu Mitra,
Apurba Roy and Suparna Kalra.**

Co-editors :
Kajal and Sangeeta

STAR CHILDREN'S PICTURE DICTIONARY

First Print (International) : December 1992
Second Print (International) : January 1993
Third Print (Indian) : January 1993

Published in India by

**STAR PUBLICATIONS PVT. LTD.
Asaf Ali Road, NEW DELHI-110 002**

sole distributors for India :

Rupa • Co

7/16, Ansari Road, Darya Ganj, New Delhi-110 002
(Branches : CALCUTTA, ALLAHABAD & BOMBAY)

**THIS PICTURE DICTIONARY
has been published in Arabic, Bengali,
Chinese, Dhivehi, Gujarati, Hindi, Punjabi, Spanish,
Tamil, Urdu and Vietnamese. Other languages are in press.**

Printed at Swan Press of Lahore, Naraina, New Delhi (India)

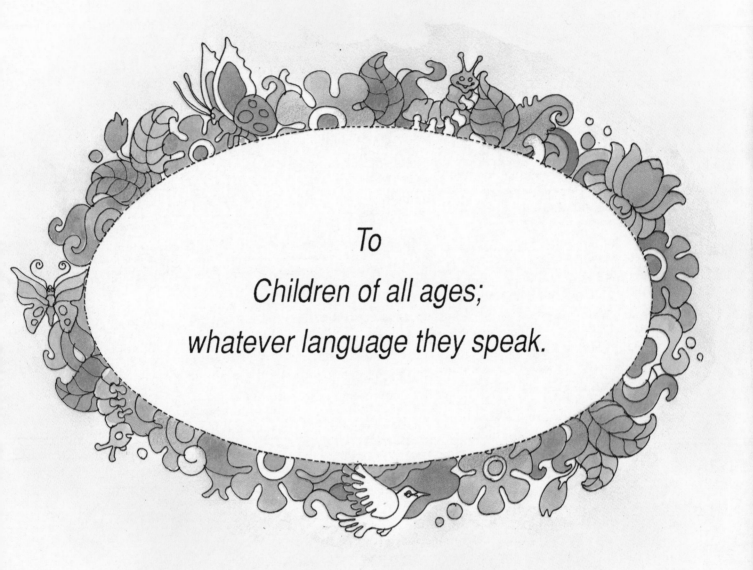

To

Children of all ages;

whatever language they speak.

FROM THE EDITOR :

This unique colourful bilingual Dictionary has been compiled for young children, to introduce them to popular words both in English and the other language, thus to help them build wordpower and stimulate learning.

The Dictionary consists of about 1,000 common words in English, arranged in alphabetical order and categorised in 14 popular subjects. Each word has been translated into the other language and has English pronunciation in roman script. A complete index in both English and the other language appears at the end of the book.

This Dictionary will have many uses—readers can have cross-reference of words from one language to the other, each word has been identified with a colourful picture, and one can enhance vocabulary in both languages to enrich conversation.

This beautifully illustrated dictionary will certainly encourage browsing, and make learning fun for the young and old alike.

As we plan to bring this dictionary in most of the modern languages of the world, if will be our timely contribution to multilingualism and multiculturalism.

December, 1992.

A a	B b	C c	D d	
E e	F f	G g	H h	I i	J j
K k	L l	M m	N n	O o	P p
Q q	R r	S s	T t	U u	V v
	W w	X x	Y y	Z z	

NUMBERS

0 零 líng

1 一 yī

2 二 er

3 三 san

4 四 sì

5 五 wǔ

6 六 liù

7 七 qī

8 八 bā

9 九 jiǔ

10 十 shí

ANIMALS BIRDS AND OTHER LIVING CREATURES

動物丶鳥類和其他生物

ant

mǎyǐ   螞蟻

ape

yuán   猿

bat

biānfú   蝙蝠

bear

xióng   熊

beetle

jiǎchóng   甲蟲

bird

niǎo   鳥

bison

yěniú   野牛

buffalo

shuǐniú   水牛

bull

gongniú   公牛

14

bustard

bǎo 鴇

butterfly

húdié 蝴蝶

calf

xiǎoniú 小牛

camel

luòtuó 駱駝

canary

jīnsīquè 金絲雀

cat

māo 貓

caterpillar

máochóng 毛蟲

centipede

wúgōng 蜈蚣

cheetah

huābào 花豹

chicken

xiǎojī 小雞

chimpanzee

hēixīngxíng 黑猩猩

cobra

yǎnjìngshé 眼鏡蛇

cock

gōngjī 公雞

cockroach

zhāngláng 蟑螂

cow

mǔniú 母牛

crab

pángxiè 螃蟹

crocodile

èyú 鱷魚

crow

wūyā 烏鴉

cub
xiǎohǔ　小虎

cuckoo
dùjuān　杜鵑

deer
lù　鹿

dinosaur
kǒnglóng　恐龍

dog
gǒu　狗

dolphin
hǎitún　海豚

donkey
lú　驢

duck
yā　鴨

eagle	elephant	falcon
yīng 鷹	**xiàng** 象	**lièyīng** 獵鷹

fish	flamingo	fly
yú 魚	**hónghè** 紅鶴	**chāngyíng** 蒼蠅

fox	frog	goat
húlí 狐狸	**qīngwā** 青蛙	**shānyáng** 山羊

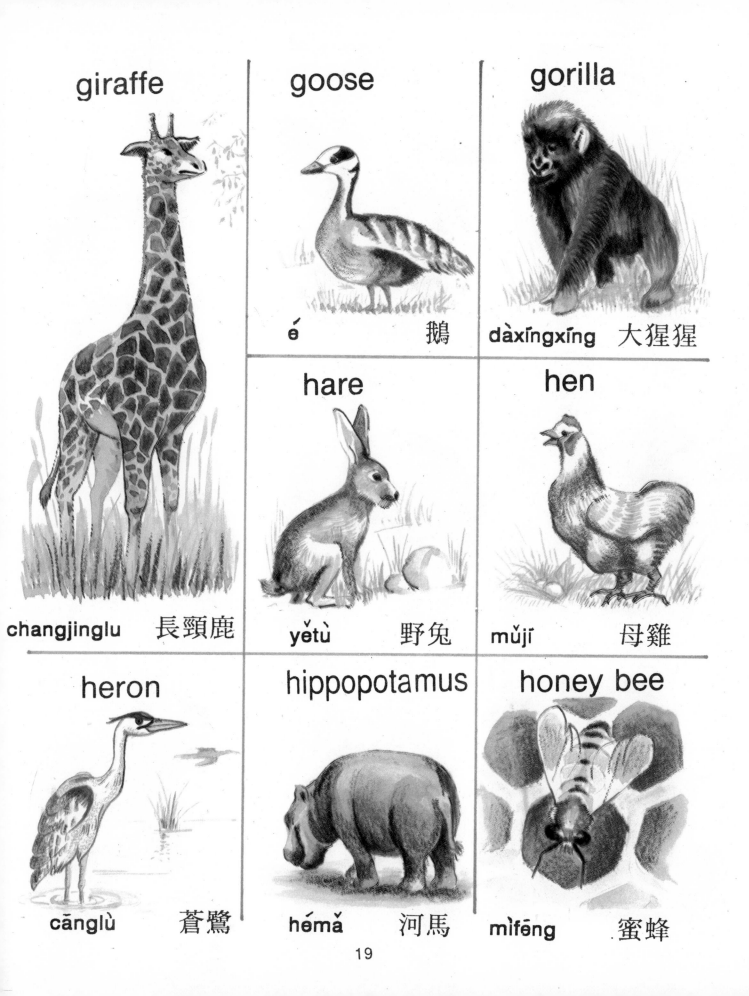

giraffe

goose

gorilla

é　　　鵝

dàxīngxīng　　大猩猩

hare

hen

changjinglu　　長頸鹿

yětù　　野兔

mǔjī　　母雞

heron

hippopotamus

honey bee

cānglù　　蒼鷺

hémǎ　　河馬

mìféng　　蜜蜂

horse

mǎ 馬

insects
kūnchóng 昆蟲

jackal
chái 豺

kangaroo
dàishǔ 袋鼠

kiwi
wúyìniǎo 無翼鳥

ladybird
piāochóng 瓢蟲

leopard
bào 豹

lion
shīzi 獅子

lizard
xīyì 蜥蜴

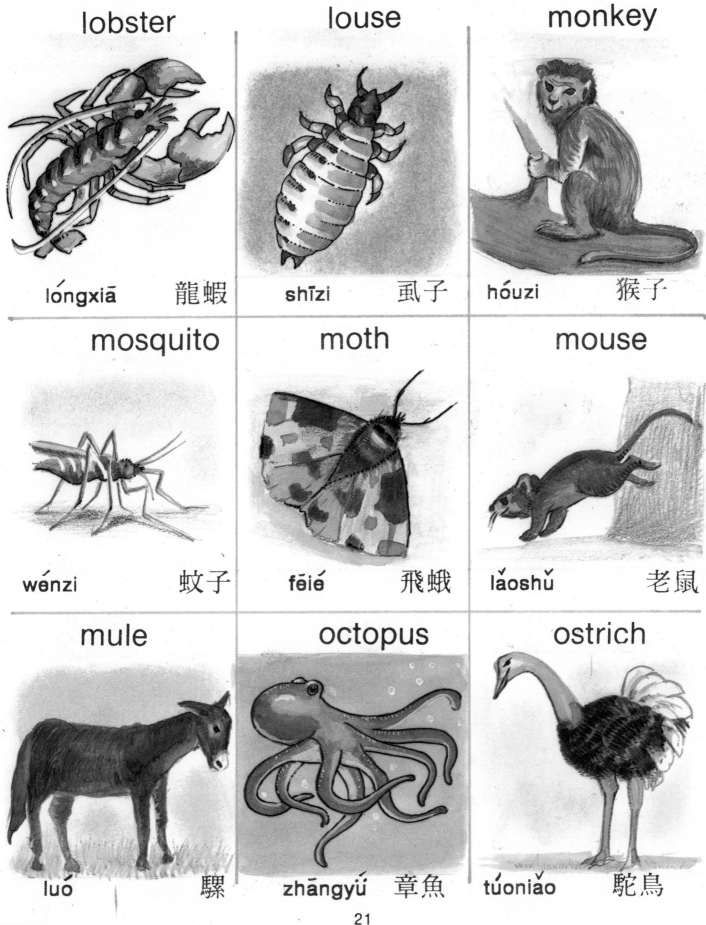

lobster	louse	monkey
lóngxiā 龍蝦	shīzi 虱子	hóuzi 猴子
mosquito	moth	mouse
wénzi 蚊子	fēié 飛蛾	lǎoshǔ 老鼠
mule	octopus	ostrich
luó 騾	zhāngyú 章魚	túoniǎo 駝鳥

otter	owl	ox
shuǐtǎ 水獺	māotóuyīng 貓頭鷹	gōngniú 公牛

panda	panther	parrot
xióngmāo 熊貓	hēibào 黑豹	yīngwǔ 鸚鵡

peacock	pelican	penguin
kǒngquè 孔雀	tángé 塘鵝	qìé 企鵝

pigeon	polar bear	pony
gēzi 鴿子	běijíxióng 北極熊	xiǎomǎ 小馬

porcupine	puppy	quail
háozhū 豪豬	xiǎogǒu 小狗	ānchún 鵪鶉

rabbit	rat	reindeer
tùzi 兔子	lǎoshǔ 老鼠	xúnlù 馴鹿

rhinoceros

xíniú   犀牛

scorpion

xiēzi   蠍子

seagull

hǎiōu   海鷗

sea horse

hǎimǎ   海馬

seal

hǎibào   海豹

shark

shāyú   鯊魚

sheep

miányáng   綿羊

snail

wōniú   窩牛

snake

shé   蛇

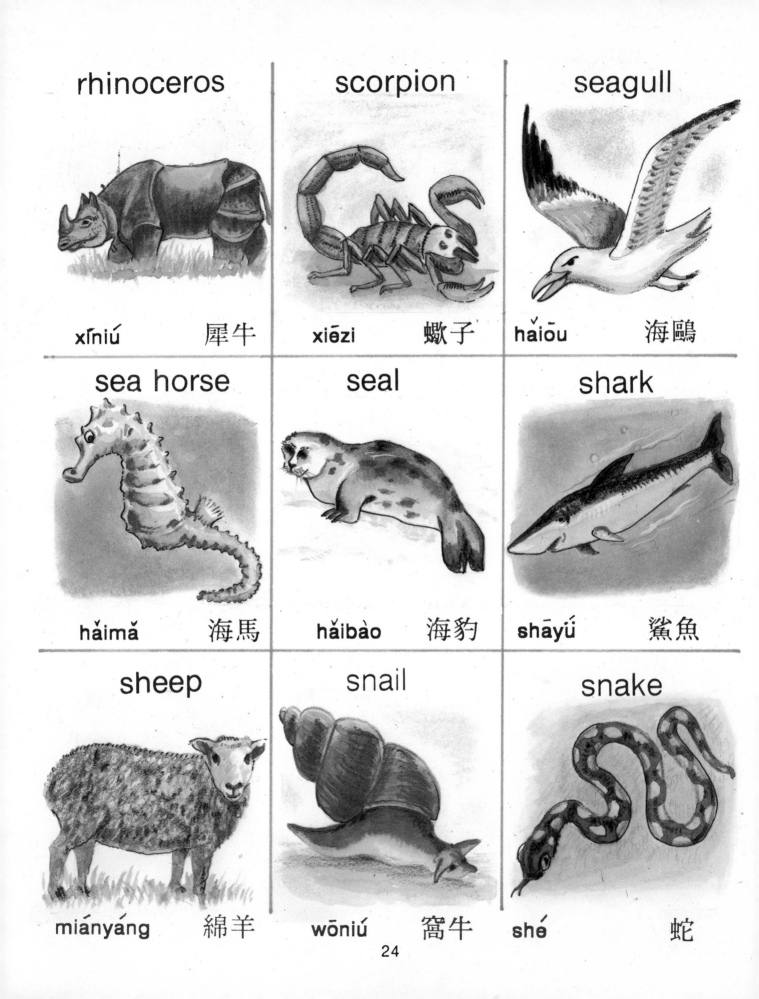

sparrow	spider	squirrel
máquè 麻雀	zhīzhū 蜘蛛	sōngshǔ 松鼠
swan	tiger	toad
tiāné 天鵝	lǎohǔ 老虎	chánchú 蟾蜍
tortoise	turkey	turtle
dàguī 大龜	huǒjī 火雞	wūguī 烏龜

vulture

tūyǐng　　禿鷹

whale

jīngyú　　鯨魚

woodpecker

zhuómùniǎo　　啄木鳥

wasp

huángfēng　　黃蜂

wolf

láng　　狼

worm

chóng　　蟲

yak

máoniú　　犛牛

zebra

bānmǎ　　斑馬

26

FOOD, DRINKS AND OTHER THINGS TO EAT

食物

almond	apple	apricot
xìngrén 杏仁	**píngguǒ** 蘋果	**xìngzi** 杏子
bananas	beans	beef
xiāngjiāo 香蕉	**dòuzi** 豆子	**niúròu** 牛肉
beetroot	biscuit	bread
tiáncài 甜菜	**bǐnggān** 餅乾	**miànbāo** 麵包

bun

xiǎoyuánmiànbāo

小圓麵包

butter

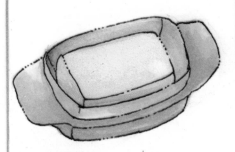

niúyóu 牛油

cabbage

juǎnxincài 捲心菜

cake

dàngāo 蛋糕

carrot

húluóbō 胡蘿蔔

cauliflower

huācài 花菜

cereal

gǔlèi 穀類

cheese

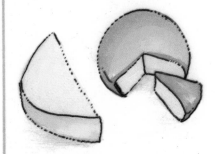

rǔluò 乳酪

cherry

yīngtáo 樱桃

chilli	chocolate	coconut

làjiāo 辣椒	qiǎokèlì 巧克力	yēzi 椰子

coffee	cucumber	currants
kāfēi 咖啡	huángguā 黄瓜	hēicùlì 黑醋栗

dates	egg	fig
zǎozi 棗子	dàn 蛋	wúhuāguǒ 無花果

fish

yú 魚

flour

miànfěn 麵粉

fruit

shuǐguǒ 水果

garlic

dàsuàn 大蒜

ginger

jiāng 薑

grapes

pútáo 葡萄

grapefruit

pútáoyòu 葡萄柚

grocery

záhuòdiàn 雜貨店

honey

fēngmì 蜂蜜

ice cream
bīngqílín 冰淇淋

jackfruit
liúlián 榴蓮

jam
guǒjiàng 果醬

jelly
guǒdòng 果凍

lamb
xiǎoyángròu 小羊肉

lemon
níngméng 檸檬

lettuce
shēngcài 生菜

loaf
miànbāo 麵包

lollipop
bàngbàngtáng 棒棒糖

32

mango

mángguǒ 芒果

meat

ròu 肉

melon

guā 瓜

milk

niúnǎi 牛奶

mushrooms

mógū 蘑菇

mustard

jièmò 芥末

mutton

yángròu 羊肉

nuts

jiānguǒ 堅果

orange

chéngzi 橙子

papaya	peach	peanuts
mùguá 木瓜	**táozi** 桃子	**huāshēng** 花生
pear	peppers	pickle
lí 梨	**làjiāo** 辣椒	**jiànggua** 醬瓜
pie	pine apple	potatoes
pāi 派	**fènglí** 鳳梨	**mǎlíngshǔ** 馬鈴薯

34

pumpkin	plums	pudding
nánguā 南瓜	lǐzi 李子	bùdīng 布丁
raddish	raisin	raspberry
luóbō 蘿蔔	pútáogān 葡萄乾	shānméi 山莓
rice	saccharine	salad
fàn 飯	tángjíng 糖精	shālā 沙拉

salt
yán 鹽

sandwich
sānmíngzhì 三明治

sauce
jiàng 醬

sausage
xiāngcháng 香腸

snacks
CHIPS
diǎnxīn 點心

soup
tāng 湯

soyabeans
huángdòu 黃豆

spaghetti
yìdàlì fěn 義大利粉

spinach
bōcài 菠菜

36

strawberry	sugar	sweet potatoes
cǎoméi 草莓	táng 糖	gānshǔ 甘薯
sweets	sweetcorn	syrup
tángguǒ 糖果	yùmǐ 玉米	tángjiāng 糖漿
tangerine	tea	toast
júzi 橘子	chá 茶	tǔsī miànbāo 吐司麵包

toffee

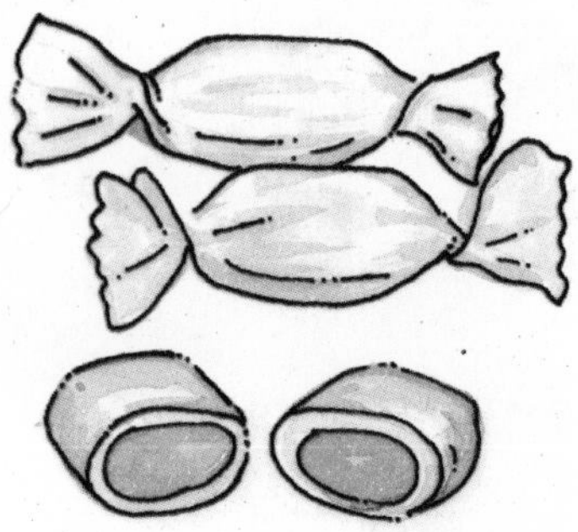

tàifēitáng 太妃糖

tomato

fānqié 番茄

turnip

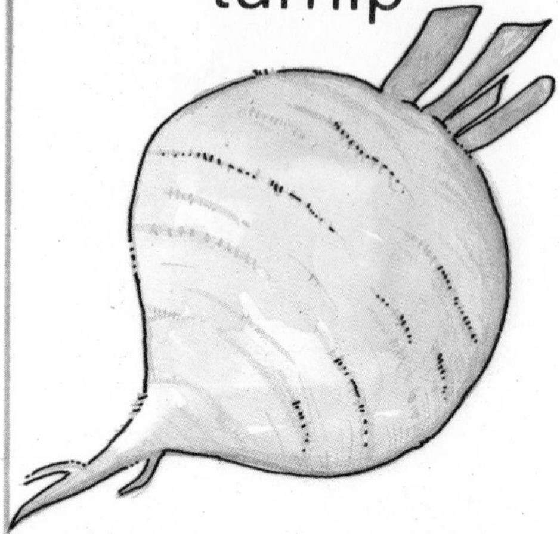

dàluóbó 大蘿蔔

vegetables

shūcài 蔬菜

walnut

hétáo 核桃

water

shuǐ 水

watermelon

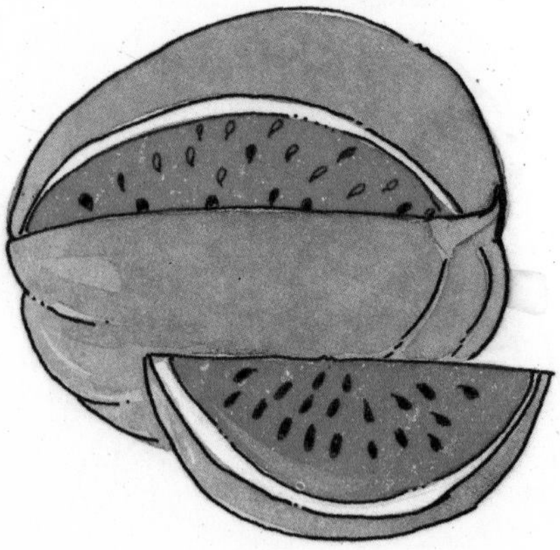

xīguā 西瓜

wheat

mài 麥

38

yoghurt

suānniúnǎi

酸牛奶

HOME

antenna
tiānxiàn　天線

almirah
guìzi　櫃子

armchair
fúshǒuyǐ　扶手椅

balcony
yángtái　陽臺

basin
xǐliǎnpén　洗臉盆

bathroom
yùshì　浴室

bed
chuáng　床

bedroom
wòfáng　臥房

bench
chángdèng　長凳

bowl

wǎn 碗

bucket

tǒng 桶

cabin

chuáncāng 船艙

cabinet

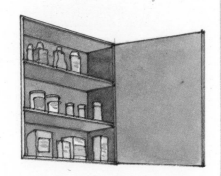

xiǎoguì 小櫃

carpet

dìtǎn 地毯

ceiling

tiānhuābǎn 天花板

chair

yǐzi 椅子

chandelier

diàodéng 吊燈

chimney

yānchóng 煙囪

cloth

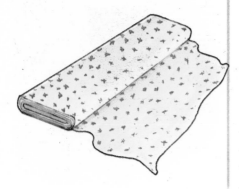

bù 布

cooker

guō 鍋

cot

yíngérchuáng 嬰兒床

cupboard

wǎnguì 碗櫃

curtain

chuānglián 窗帘

door

mén 門

drain

páishuǐdào 排水道

dressing table

shūzhuāngtái 梳妝臺

elevator

diàntī 電梯

escalator

fúshǒu diàntī 扶手電梯

fence

líbā 籬笆

flower vase

huāpíng 花瓶

foam

hǎimián 海綿

fork

chāzi 叉子

furniture

jiājù 傢俱

garden

huāyuán 花園

garage

chēfáng 車房

gate

dàmén 大門

home

jiā 家

hose

shuǐguǎn 水管

kitchen

chúfáng 廚房

letter box

xìnxiāng 信箱

mattress

chuángdiàn 床墊

mop

tuōbǎ 拖把

necktie

lǐngdài 領帶

oven

kǎoxiāng 烤箱

pan

píngdǐguō 平底鍋

plate

pánzi　盤子

pram

yīngérchē　嬰兒車

roof

wūdǐng　屋頂

rug

xiǎodìtǎn　小地毯

seat

zuòwèi　座位

shelf

bìchú　壁櫥

shower

línyù　淋浴

sink

shuǐcáo　水槽

smoke

yān　煙

sofa	steps	tap
shāfā 沙發	jiētī 階梯	shuǐlóngtóu 水龍頭

toilet	tooth brush	tub
mǎtǒng 馬桶	yāshuā 牙刷	yùgāng 浴缸

wall	wardrobe	window
qiáng 牆	yīguì 衣櫃	chuāng 窗

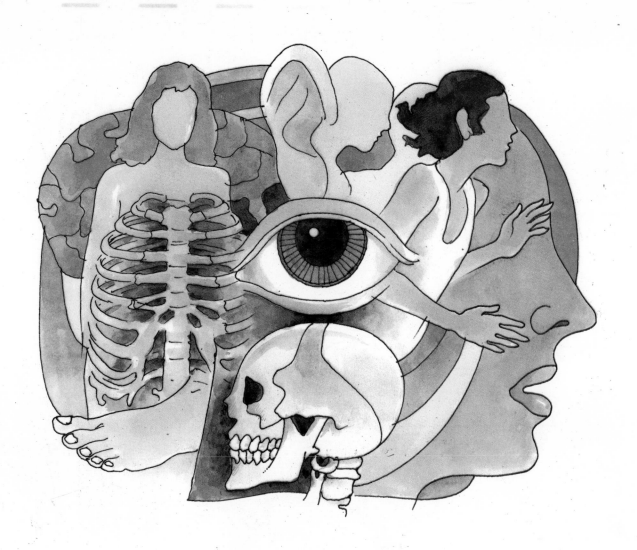

HUMAN BODY

人體

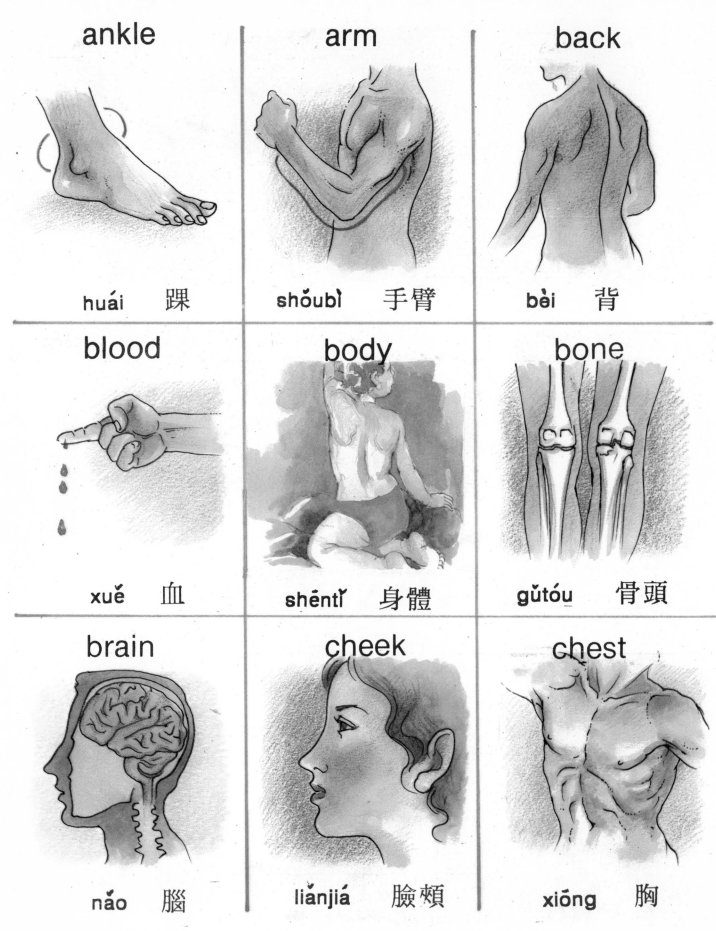

ankle	arm	back
huái 踝	shǒubì 手臂	bèi 背
blood	body	bone
xuě 血	shēntǐ 身體	gǔtóu 骨頭
brain	cheek	chest
nǎo 腦	liǎnjiá 臉頰	xiōng 胸

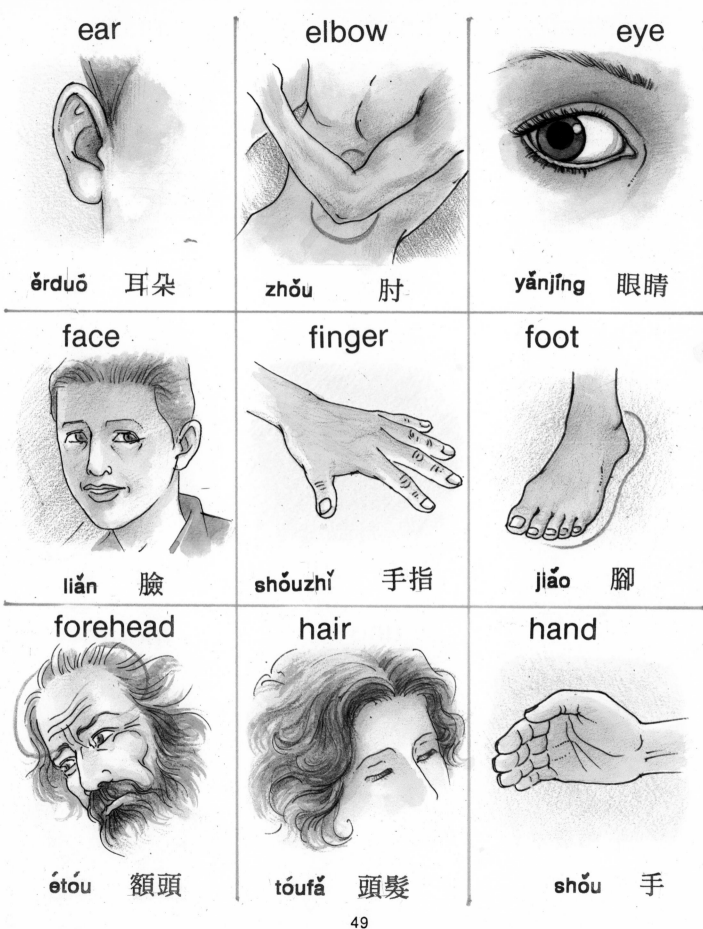

ear **ěrduǒ** 耳朵	elbow **zhǒu** 肘	eye **yǎnjíng** 眼睛
face **liǎn** 臉	finger **shǒuzhǐ** 手指	foot **jiǎo** 腳
forehead **étóu** 額頭	hair **tóufǎ** 頭髮	hand **shǒu** 手

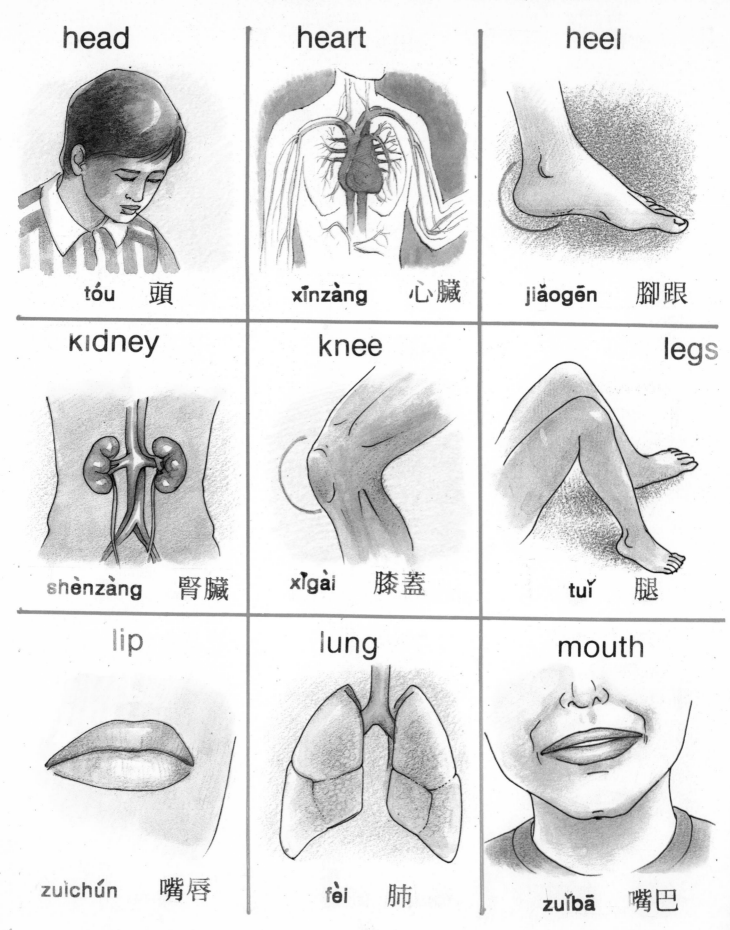

head
tóu 頭

heart
xīnzàng 心臟

heel
jiǎogēn 腳跟

kidney
shènzàng 腎臟

knee
xīgài 膝蓋

legs
tuǐ 腿

lip
zuìchún 嘴唇

lung
fèi 肺

mouth
zuǐbā 嘴巴

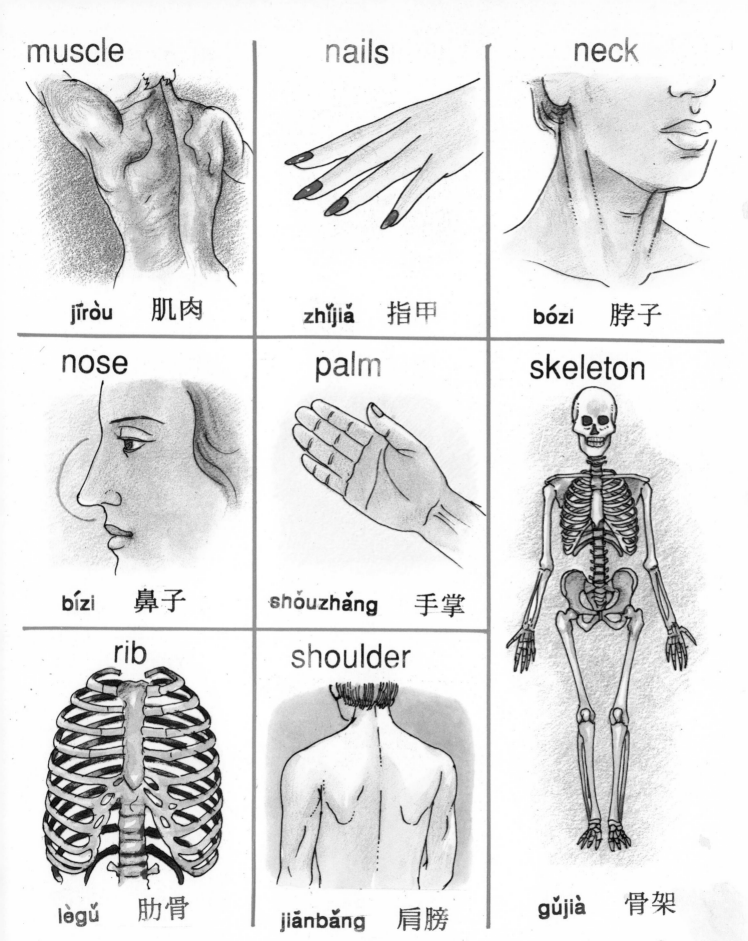

muscle

jīròu　肌肉

nails

zhǐjiǎ　指甲

neck

bózi　脖子

nose

bízi　鼻子

palm

shǒuzhǎng　手掌

skeleton

gǔjià　骨架

rib

lèigú　肋骨

shoulder

jiānbǎng　肩膀

51

skin

pífū　皮膚

skull

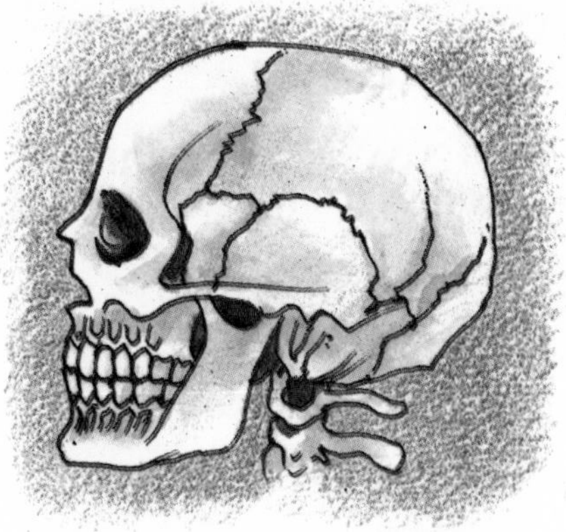

tóugǔ　頭骨

stomach

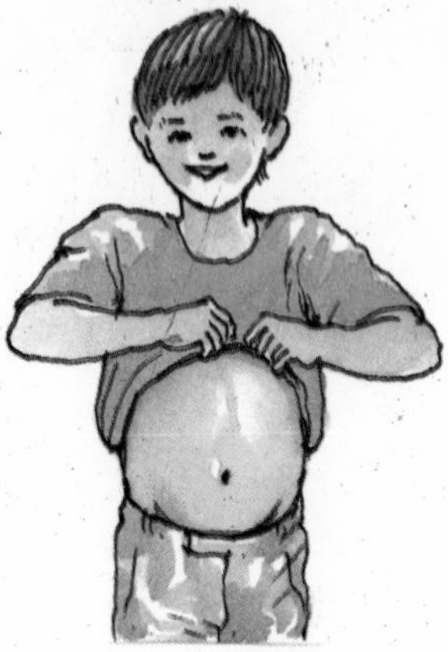

dǔzi　肚子

teeth

yáchǐ　牙齒

throat

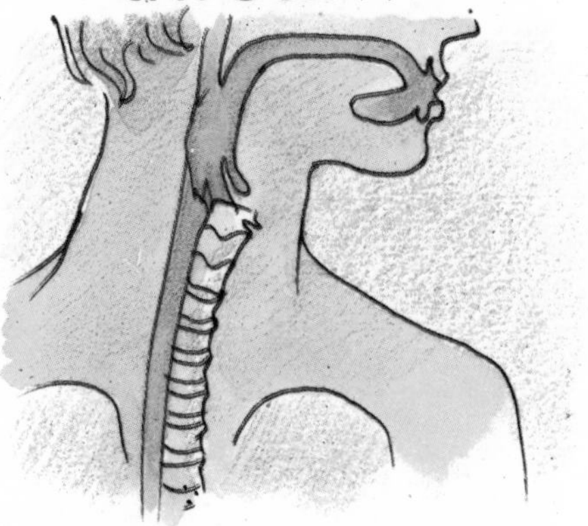

hóulóng　喉嚨

thumb

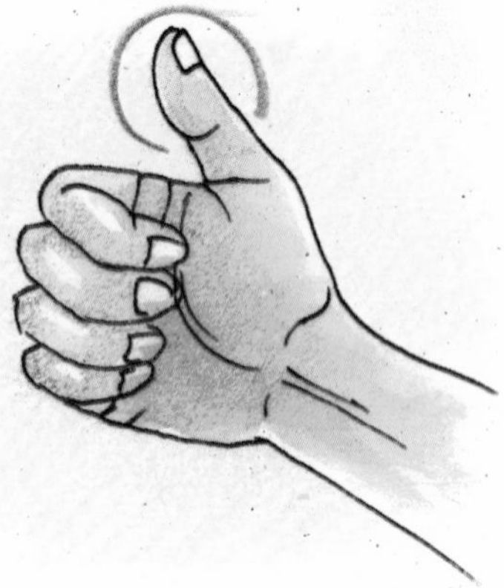

múzhǐ　拇指

tongue

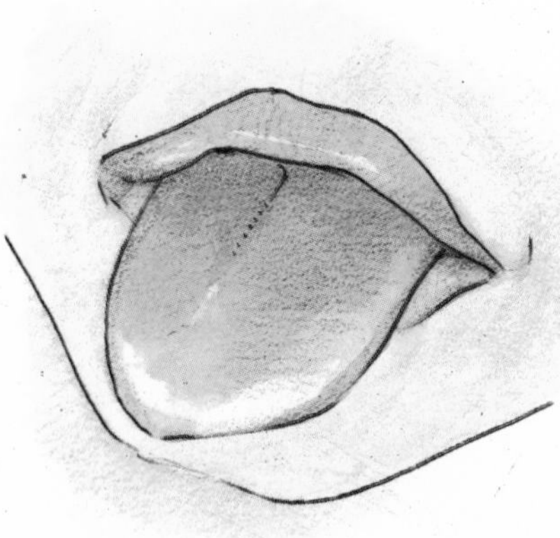

shétóu　舌頭

waist

yāo　腰

wrist

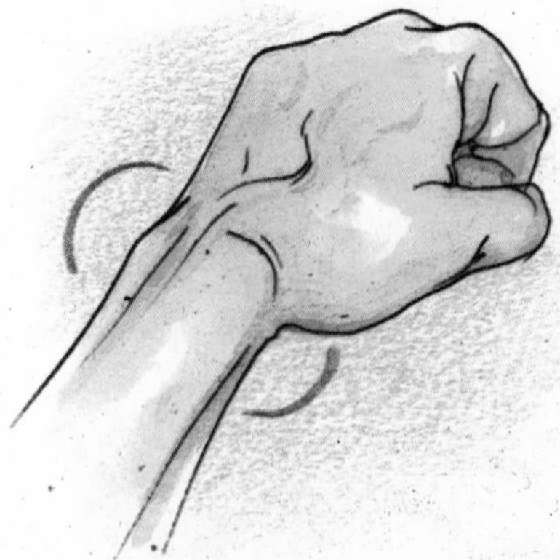

shǒuwǎn　手腕

MEASUREMENTS, SHAPES, COLOURS AND TIME

度量衡、形狀、顏色和時間

black	blue	brown
hēi 黑	lán 藍	zōng 棕
circle	cone	cube
yuán 圓	yuánzhuǐ 圓錐	lìfāng 立方
decimal	green	heap
xiǎoshù 小數	lù 綠	duī 堆

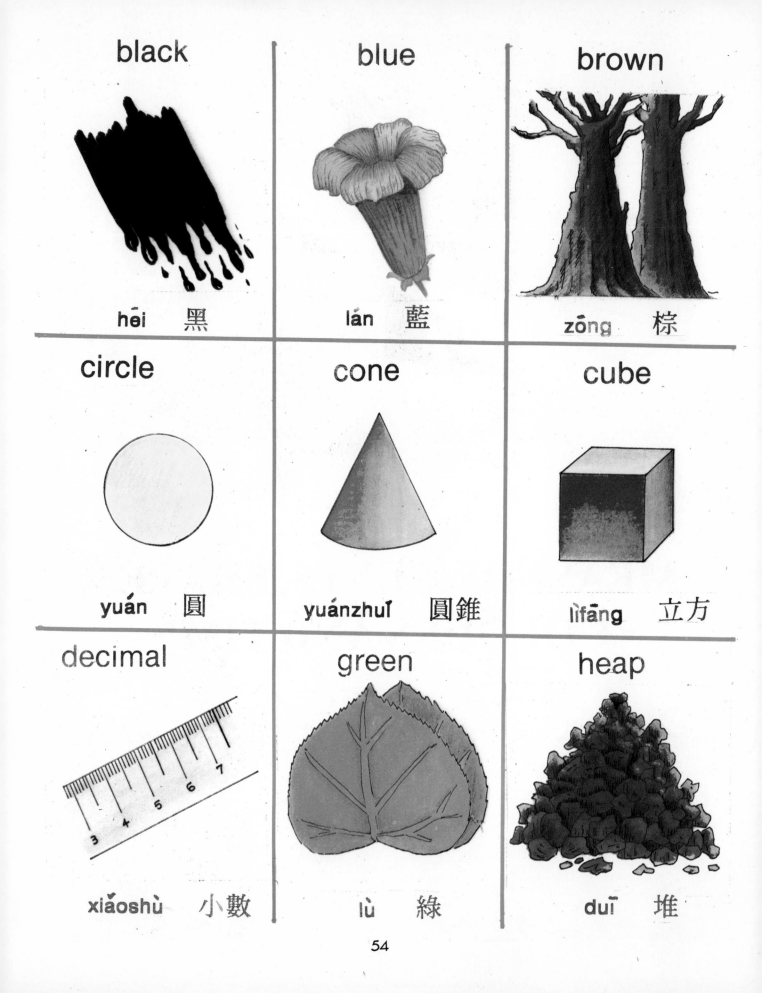

heavy

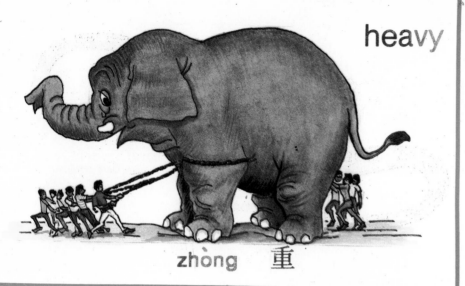

zhòng　重

height

gáo　高

high

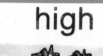

gāodù　高度

kilogram

gōngjīn　公斤

length

chángdù　長度

large

dà　大

litre

gōngshéng　公升

little

xiǎo 小

long

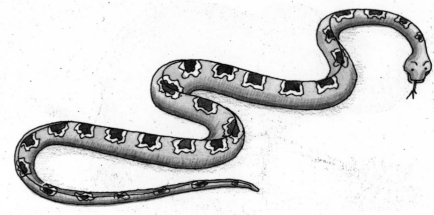

cháng 長

low

dī 低

metre

gōngchǐ 公尺

mile

yīnglǐ 英里

minute

fēnzhōng 分鐘

month

yuè 月

orange

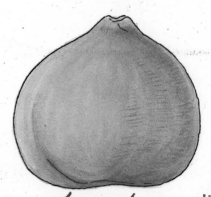

chénghuáng 橙黃

oval

tuǒyuán 橢圓

pair

shuāng 雙

pink

fěnhóng 粉紅

rectangle

chángfāngxíng
長方形

red

hóng 紅

small

xiǎo 小

square

zhèngfāngxíng
正方形

sphere

yuán 圓

tall

gāo 高

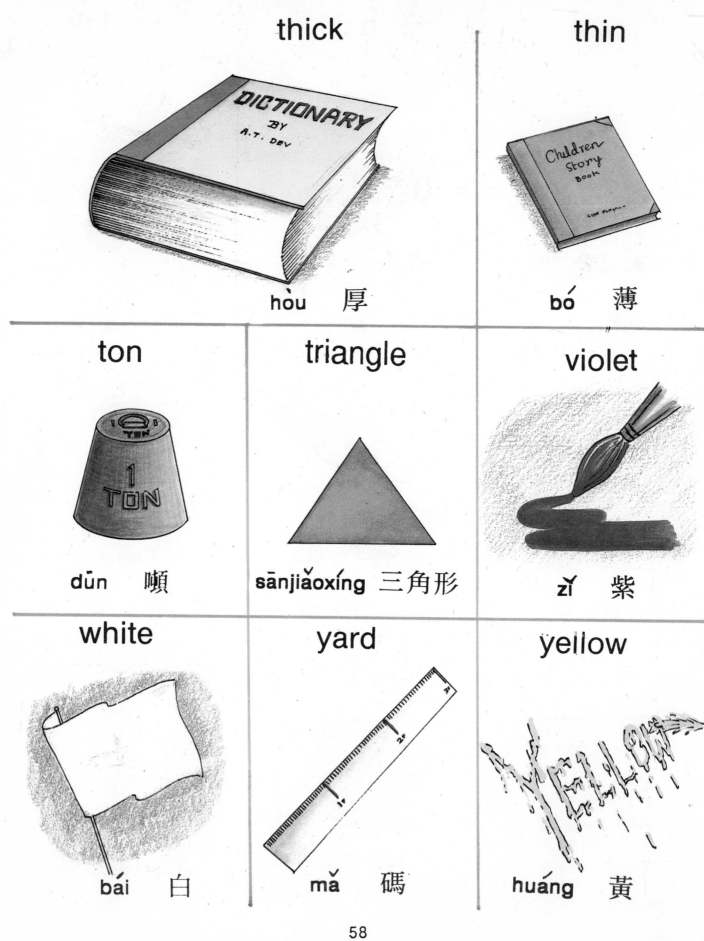

thick	thin
hòu 厚	bó 薄

ton	triangle	violet
dūn 噸	sānjiǎoxíng 三角形	zǐ 紫

white	yard	yellow
bái 白	mǎ 碼	huáng 黃

PEOPLE, COSTUMES AND ORNAMENTS

人物衣著

actor

nán yǎnyuán 男演員

actress

nǚyǎnyuán 女演員

adult

chénrén 成人

angel

tiānshǐ 天使

architect

jiànzhúshī 建築師

artist

yìshùjiā 藝術家

astronaut

tàikōngrén 太空人

athlete

yùndòngyuán 運動員

author

zuòjiā 作家

baby

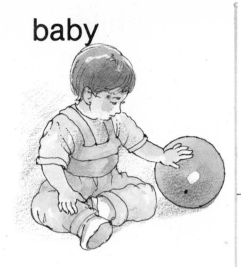

yīngér 嬰兒

baker

gāobǐngshī 糕餅師

bandit

qiángdào 强盗

bishop

zhǔjiào 主教

blacksmith

tiějiàng 鐵匠

boy

nánhái 男孩

bride

xīnniáng 新娘

bridegroom

xīnláng 新郎

brother

xiōngdì 兄弟

captain

chuánzhǎng 船長

carpenter

mùjiàng 木匠

child

háizi 孩子

clown

xiǎochǒu 小丑

conductor

chēzhǎng 車掌

cook/chef

chúshì 廚師

crowd

qúnzhòng 群眾

dancers

wǔdǎojiā 舞蹈家

daughter

nǚér 女兒

dentist

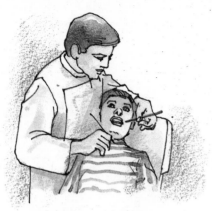

yáyī 牙醫

doctor

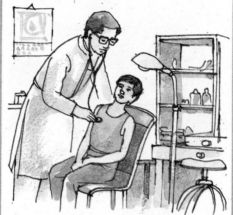

yīshēng 醫生

driver

sījī 司機

dwarf

zhūrú 侏儒

electrician

diàngōng 電工

family

jiātíng 家庭

farmer

nóngrén 農人

father

fùqin 父親

fire fighter

xiāofángyuán 消防員

girl

nǔhái 女孩

grand child

sunzi 孫子

grand father

zǔfù 祖父

grand mother

zǔmǔ 祖母

husband

zhàngfū 丈夫

infant

yòuér 幼兒

king

guówáng 國王

knight

wǔshì 武士

lady

nǔshì 女士

64

man

nánrén 男人

mechanic

jīxièshī 機械師

miner

kuànggōng 礦工

merchant

shāngrén 商人

monk

héshàng 和尚

musician

yīnyuèjiā 音樂家

mother

mǔqín 母親

nephew

zhízi 侄子

niece

zhínǔ 侄女

nun

xiōunǚ 修女

nurse

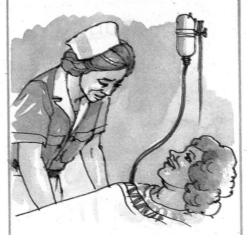

hùshì 護士

painter

yóuqijiàng 油漆匠

people

rén 人

pilot

fēixíngyuán 飛行員

plumber

shuǐhóujiàng 水喉匠

policeman

jǐngchá 警察

porter

bānyùngóng 搬運工

postman

yóuchāi 郵差

priest

jiàoshì 教士

prince

wángzǐ 王子

queen

wánghòu 王后

robber

qiángdào 强盗

sailor

shuǐshǒu 水手

saint

shèngrén 聖人

shepherd

mùrén 牧人

shopkeeper

diànzhǔ 店主

sisters

jiěmèi 姊妹

soldier

jūnrén 軍人

solicitor

lùshī 律師

son

érzi 兒子

teacher

jiàoshī 教師

thief

zéi 賊

waiter

zhāodài 招待

wife

qīzǐ 妻子

woman

nǚrén 女人

wrestlers

shuāijiāoshǒu 摔跤手

PLACES AND BUILDINGS

地方和建築物

apartment

gōngyù 公寓

airport

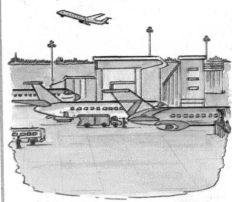

fēijīchǎng 飛機場

bank

yínháng 銀行

bay

hǎiwán 海灣

bazaar

shìjí 市集

beach

hǎitān 海灘

bridge

qiáo 橋

bungalow

biéshù 別墅

cafe

kāfēiguǎn   咖啡館

camp

lùyíng   露營

canal

yùnhé   運河

castle

chéngbǎo   城堡

cathedral

dà jiàotáng   大教堂

cave

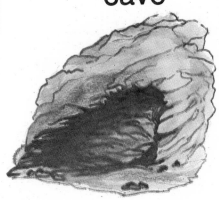

shāndòng   山洞

church

jiàotáng   教堂

cinema

diànyǐngyuàn   電影院

city

chéngshì   城市

71

circus

mǎxìtuán 馬戲團

clinic

zhěnsuǒ 診所

coast

hǎiàn 海岸

college

xuéyuàn 學院

corner

zhuǎnjiǎo 轉角

cottage

cūnshè 村舍

country

xiāngcūn 鄉村

court

fǎtíng 法庭

den

shòuxuè 獸穴

desert

SHA MÒ 沙漠

dome

YUÁN DING 圓頂

exhibition

ZHAN LAN
展覽

factory

GÖNG CHANG
工廠

farm

NONG CHANG
農場

field

TIÁN YE 田野

forest

SÊN LÍN 森林

fort

BAO LEI 堡壘

gallery

HUÀ LANG
畫廊

garage

CHĒ FANG 車房

garden

HUA YUAN 花園 园

glacier

BING HÉ 冰河

gulf

HAI WÀN 海灣

hospital

YĪ YUÀN 醫院

hostel

SÙ SHÈ 宿舍

hotel

LU GUAN 旅館

house

FÁNG ZI 房子

inn

GŌNG YÙ 公寓

island

DAO 島

jungle

HUĀNG YE 荒野

kiosk

XIAO MÀI TÍNG

小賣亭

laboratory

SHÍ YÀN SHÌ

實驗室

lake

HU 湖

lane

XIÀNG ZI 巷子

library

TÚ SHÜ GUAN

圖書館

light house

DĔNG TA 燈塔

market

SHÌ CHANG 市場

monument

JI NIAN BEI

紀念碑

mosque

QING ZHEN SI 清真寺

mountain

SHAN 山

museum

BO WU GUAN 博物館

observatory

TIAN WEN TAI

天文臺

ocean

HAI YÁNG 海洋

office

辦公室

BAN GONG SHI

orchard

果園

GUO YUAN

palace

GONG DIAN 宮殿

park

GONG YUAN 公園

pavement

RÉN XÍNG DAO
人行道

pillar

ZHÙ ZI 柱子

platform

TÁI JIÀ 臺架

play ground

YÓU XÌ CHANG
游戲場

pond

CHÍ TÁNG 池塘

pool

SHUI CHÍ 水池

port

HAI GANG 海港

post office

YÓU JÚ 郵局

prison

JIAN YÙ 監獄

restaurant

FÀN GUAN 飯館

river

HÉ 河

road

LÙ 路

school

XUÉ XIÀO 學校

sky scraper

shed

PÉNG 棚

shop
SHANG DIÀN 商店

MÓ TIAN DÀ LÓU 摩天大樓

stadium

YUN DONG CHANG

運動場

stage

WU TAI

舞臺

station

HUO CHE ZHAN

火車站

street

JIE 街

subway

DI DAO 也道

supermarket

CHAO JI SHI CHANG

超級市場

swimming pool

YOU YONG CHI 游泳池

temple

MIAO 廟

theatre

JU CHANG

劇場

tower

GAO LOU 高樓

town

CHENG ZHÈN 城鎮

tunnel

SUÌ DAO 隧道

university

DÀ XUÉ 大學

valley

SHAN GU 山谷

verandah

WAÌ LÁNG 外廊

village

CUN ZI 村子

ward

BÌNG FÁNG 病房

zoo

DONG WU YUAN
動物園

PLANTS AND FLOWERS

植物花草

acorn

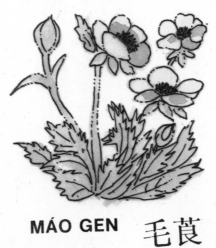

XIANG ZI 橡子

alder

CHI YANG 赤楊

balsam

XIANG JIAO SHU
香膠樹

bamboo

ZHU

birch

HUA SHU 樺樹

branch

SHU ZHI 樹枝

bush

SHU CONG
樹叢

buttercup

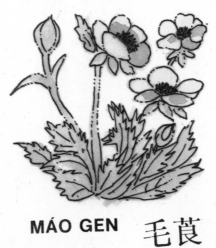

MÁO GEN 毛茛

cactus

仙人掌
XIAN RÉN ZHANG

carnation

SHÈ XIANG SHI ZHÚ 麝香石竹

corn

YU SHU SHU 玉蜀黍

cotton

MIAN 棉

daffodil

HUANG SHUI XIAN 黃水仙

daisy

CHU JU 雛菊

dandelion

PÚ GONG YING 蒲公央

egg plant

QIE 茄

elm

YÚ SHÙ aabel

fern

JUE 蕨

carnation

SHA SHU 杉樹

corn

YA MA 亞麻

cotton

LAO GUÀN CAO

老鸛草

grass

CAO 草

heliopsis

KUI HUA 葵花

hollyhock

CUI QUE HUA 崔雀化

honeysuckle

REN DONG 忍冬

hyacinth

FENG XIN ZI 風信子

iris

YUAN WEI

鳶尾

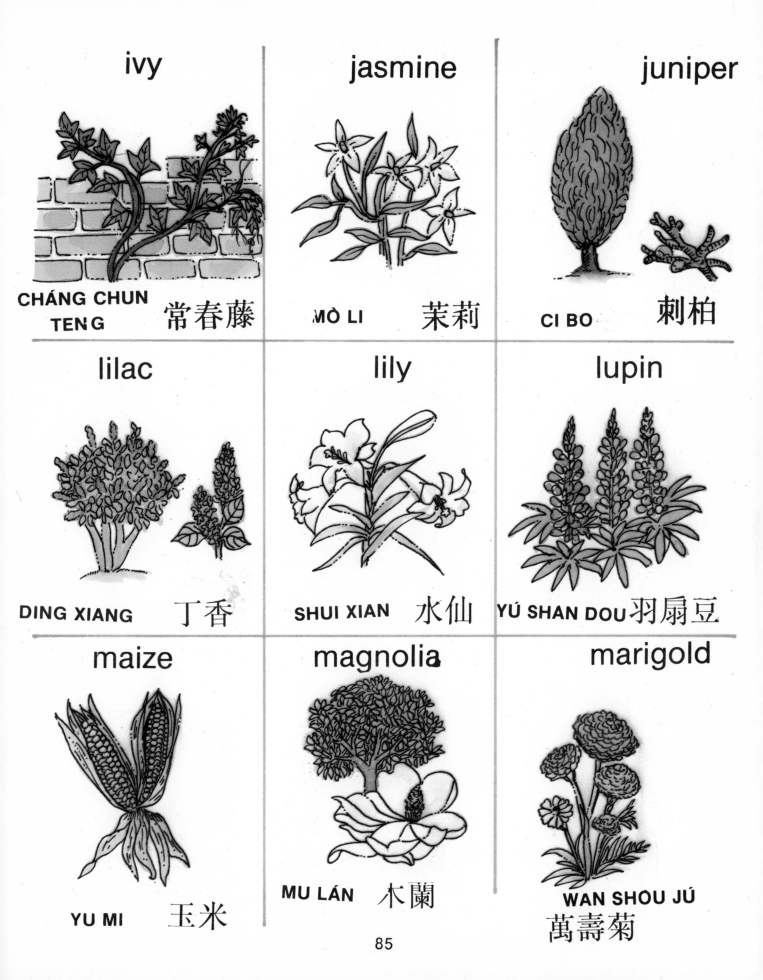

ivy

CHÁNG CHUN TEN G 常春藤

jasmine

MÒ LI 茉莉

juniper

CI BO 刺柏

lilac

DING XIANG 丁香

lily

SHUI XIAN 水仙

lupin

YÚ SHAN DOU 羽扇豆

maize

YU MI 玉米

magnolia

MU LÁN 木蘭

marigold

WAN SHOU JÚ 萬壽菊

narcissus

SHUI XIAN 水仙

nasturtium

SHUI TIAN JIE

水田芥

oak

LI SHÙ 櫟樹

oat

YAN MAI 燕麥

olive

GAN LAN 橄欖

onion

YÁNG CONG 洋葱

orchid

LAN HUA 蘭花 兰)

palm-tree

棕樹

ZONG SHU 86

parsley

OU QIN 歐芹

peas

QING DOU 青豆

peony

MU DAN 牡丹

redwood

HÓNG SHA 紅杉

root

GEN 根

rose

MEI GUI 玫瑰

sage

SHU WEI CAO 鼠尾草

shamrock

SAN YE CAO
三葉草

sugarcane

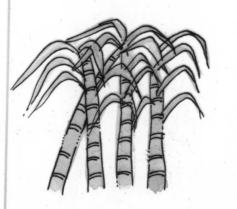

GAN ZHE 甘蔗

sunflower

XIÀNG RI KUÍ 向日葵

thorn

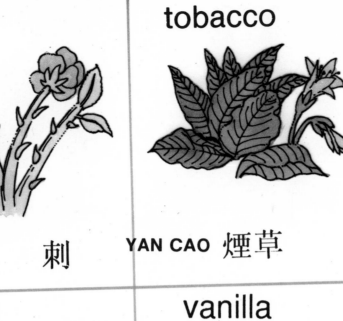

CI 刺

tobacco

YAN CAO 煙草

tree

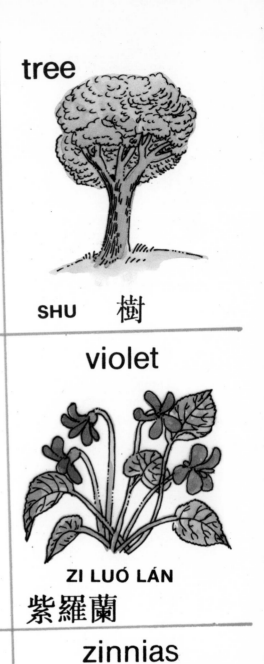

SHU 樹

tulip

YU JIN XIANG

鬱金香

vanilla

XIANG GUO LAN

香果蘭

violet

ZI LUÓ LÁN

紫羅蘭

waterlily

SHUI LIAN

睡蓮

yam

YU 芋

zinnias

BAI RÌ JU 百日菊

SPORTS, GAMES AND RECREATION

運動遊戲

arrow

JIÀN 箭

badminton

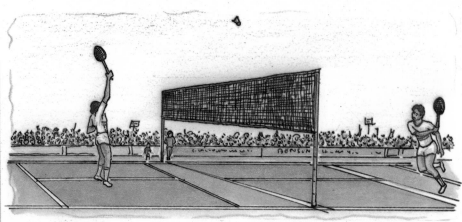

YÚ MÁO QIÚ 羽毛球

ball

QIÚ 球

ballet

BA LEI WU 芭蕾舞

balloon

QÌ QIU 氣球

basket ball

LÁN QIU 籃球

bat

QIU BANG 球棒

billiard

ZHUO QIÚ 桌球

bull fight

DOÙ NIÚ 鬥牛

carrom board

KÈ LANG QÍ 克郎棋

chess

XIÀNG QÍ 象棋

clarinet

DAN HUANG GUAN

單簧管

cornet

DUAN HÀO

短號 ㄅ

cricket

drum

GU 鼓

flute

DI 笛

BAN QIU 板球

football

ZÚ QIÚ 足球

golf

GAO ER FU QIU

高爾夫球

guitar

JÍ TA QIN 吉他琴

hockey

QU GÙN QIÚ 曲棍球

kite

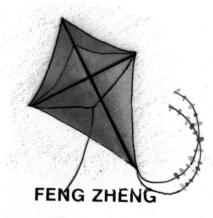

FENG ZHENG

風箏

mandolin

PÍ PA 琵琶

organ

FENG QIN 風琴

piano	puppet	racket
GANG QÍN 鋼琴	KUI LEI XI 傀儡戲	QIÚ PAI 球拍
see-saw	shuttle-cock	sitar
QIAO BAN 蹺板	YÚ MAO QIÚ 羽毛球	XT IA QÍN 西塔琴
skates	ski	swing
LIU BING XIÉ 溜冰鞋	HUÁ XUE 滑雪	QIU QIAN 秋千

tennis

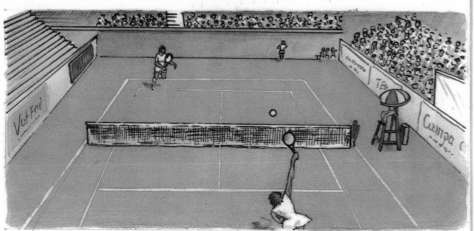

WANG QIÚ 網球

toy

WAN JU 玩具

trumpet

LA BA 喇叭

violin

XIAO TÍ QÍN 小提琴

volley ball

PAÍ QIÚ 排球

wicket

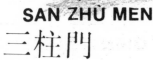

SAN ZHÙ MEN
三柱門

xylo phone

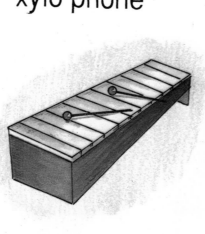

MÙ QIN 木琴

TRANSPORT
AND
COMMUNICATION

交通通訊

aeroplane

FEI JI

飛機

ambulance

JIÙ HÙ CHE

救護車

automobile

QÌ CHE 汽車

axle

ZHÓU 軸

bicycle

ZÌ XÍNG CHE

自行車

boat

CHUAN 船

bus

GONG GÒNG QI CHE

公共汽車

car

XIAO QÌ CHE

小汽車

caravan

ZHÙ SÙ CHE

住宿車

cart

SHOU TUI CHE

手推車

coach

DÀ KÈ CHE

大客車

crane

DIÀO CHE 吊車

engine

HUO CHE TÓU

火車頭

fax

CHUÁN ZHEN

傳真

generator

發電機 **FA DIÀN JI**

glider

HUÁ XIÁNG JI

滑翔機

helicopter

ZHÍ SHENG JI

直升機

hovercraft

QÌ DIÀN CHUÁN

氣墊船

jeep

JÍ PU　吉普

letter

XIN　信

motor cycle

MÓ TUO CHE　摩托車

parachute

JIÀNG LUÒ SAN　降落傘

petrolpump

JÍA YÓU ZHÀN　加油站

postcard

MÍNG XIN PIÀN　明信片

raft

MÙ FÁ　木筏

radio

SHOU YIN JI　收音機

scooter

輕機動車

QING JI DÒNG CHE

ship

CHUÁN 船

signal

XÌN HAO 信號

sledge

XUE QIAO 雪橇

stamp

YÓU PIÀO 郵票

submarine

QIÁN TING 潛艇

tanker

YÓU CHE 油車

taxi

JÌ CHÉNG CHE
計程車

telephone

DIÀN HUÀ
電話

television

DÍAN SHÌ
電視

telex

DIÀN CHUÁN

電傳

tractor

TUO LA JI

拖拉機

train

HUO CHE

火車

tramcar

DIÀN CHE

電車

van

XI ANG SHÌ QÌ CHE

廂式汽車

vehicle

CHE LIÀNG

車輛

wagon

CHE PÍ 車皮

wheel

LÚN 輪

yacht

FAN CHUÁN 帆船

UNIVERSE AND WEATHER

宇宙氣候

antarctica
NÁN JÍ 南極

arctic
BEI JÍ 北極

atom
YUÁN ZI 原子

autumn
QIU TIAN 秋天

avalanche
XUE BENG 雪崩

blizzard
BÀO FENG XUE 暴風雪

cloud
YÚN 雲

comet
HUÌ XING 彗星

dew	drought	earth
LÙ 露	HÀN ZAI 旱災	DÌ QIÚ 地球

earthquake	eclipse	flood
DÌ ZHÈN 地震	SHÍ 蝕	SHUI ZAI 水災

fog	globe	horizon
WÙ 霧	DÌ QIÚ 地球	DÌ PÍNG XIÀN 地平綫

lightning
SHAN DIÀN 閃電

map
DÌ TÚ 地圖

moon
YUÈ LIÀNG 月亮

orbit
軌道

planet
XÍNG XING 行星

rain
YU 雨

rainbow
HÓNG 虹

satellite
RÉN ZÀO WÈI XING 人造衛星

saturn
TU XING 土星

104

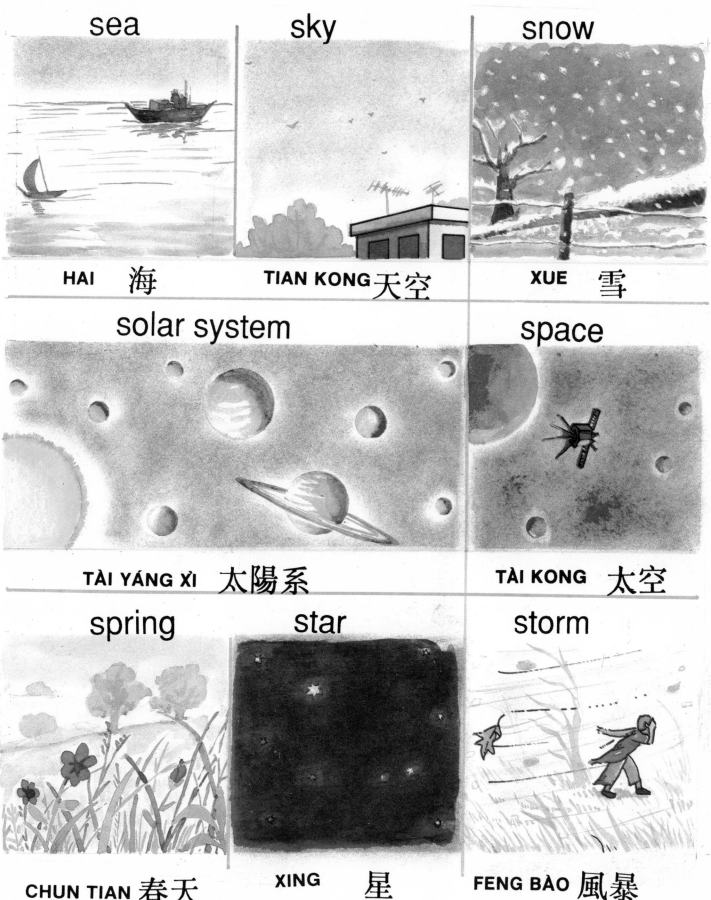

sea
HAI 海

sky
TIAN KONG 天空

snow
XUE 雪

solar system
TÀI YÁNG XÌ 太陽系

space
TÀI KONG 太空

spring
CHUN TIAN 春天

star
XING 星

storm
FENG BÀO 風暴

summer

XIÀ TIAN 夏天

sun

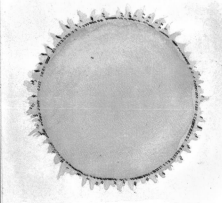

TÀI YÁNG 太陽

thunder

LÉI 雷

tornado

XUÀN FENG BÀO

旋風暴

typhoon

颱風 TÁI FENG

volcano

HUO SHAN 火山

winter

DONG TIAN 冬天

OTHER USEFUL WORDS

其他

adhesive

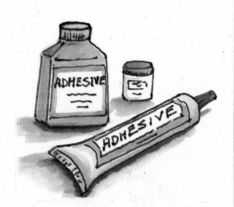

黏劑 **NIÁN JÌ**

album

ZHÀO XIANG BEN
照相本

ammunition

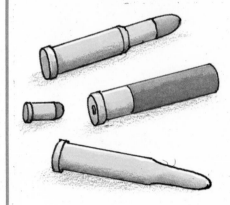

彈藥 **DÀN YÀO**

atlas

DÌ TÚ CÈ
地圖册

axe

FU TÓU 斧頭

badge

HUI ZHANG 徽章

bag

DÀI ZI 袋子

barrel

TONG 桶

baskets

LÁN ZI 籃子

battery

DIÀN CHÍ 電池

bells

LÍNG 鈴

blades

DAO PIÀN 刀片

bomb

ZHÀ DÀN 炸彈

book

SHŪ 書

bottles

PÍNG ZI 瓶子

box

HÉ ZI 盒子

brick

ZHUAN 磚

brushes

SHUA ZI 刷子

belt
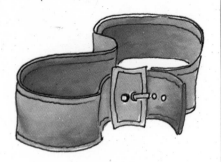
YAO DÀI 腰帶

buttons

KÒU ZI 扣子

cable

電纜 **DIÀN LÀN**

cage

LÓNG ZI 籠子

camera

ZHÀO XIANG JI
照相機

candle

LÀ ZHÚ
蠟燭

cards (playing)

ZHI PAI 紙牌

chain

LIÀN TIÁO
鏈條

cheque

ZHI PIÀO 支票

coal

MÉI 煤

coins

QIAN BÌ 錢幣

comb

SHU ZI 梳子

computer

電腦 **DIÀN NAO**

cord

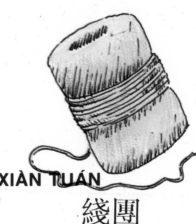

XIÀN TUÁN

綫團

cushion

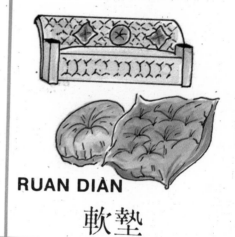

RUAN DIÀN

軟墊

cylinder

TONG 筒

dagger

BI SHOU 匕首

desk

書桌

SHU ZHUO

111

dish

PÀN ZI 盤子

drawer

CHOU TI 抽屜

drugs

YÀO 藥

dustbin

USE ME

LA JI XIANG 垃圾箱

envelope

XIN FENG 信封

eraser

ERASER

XIÀNG PÍ 橡皮

fans

SHÀN 扇

fire

HUO 火

flag

QÍ 旗

112

fountain

EN SHUI CHÍ 噴水池

fur

QIU 裘

garbage

LA JI 垃圾

gift

LI WÙ 禮物

glass

BO LI 玻璃

gloves

SHOU TÀO 手套

goblet

AO JIAO BEI 高腳杯

goggles

YAN JING 眼鏡

gum/glue

JIAO SHUI 膠水

guns

QIANG PÀO 槍炮

hammer

CHUÍ ZI 槌子

handkerchief

SHOU PÀ 手帕

handle

BA BING 把柄

hats

MÀO ZI 帽子

helmet

TÓU KUI 頭盔

ink

MÒ SHUI 墨水

ivory

XIÀNG YA 象牙

jar

TÁN 罈

jug

GUÀN ZI 罐子

kettle

SHUI HU 水壺（壶）

keys

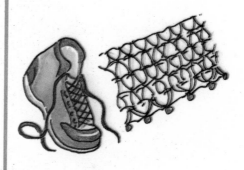

YÀO SHÌ 鑰匙（钥）

knife

DAO ZI 刀子

label

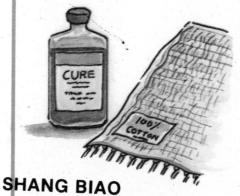

SHANG BIAO

商標（标）

lace

XIÉ DÀI 鞋帶（带）

ladder

TI ZI 梯子

leather

PÍ 皮

lens

TÒU JÌNG

透鏡（透镜）

letter

XÌN 信

lock

SUO 鎖

luggage

XÍNG LI 行李

machine

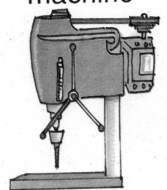

JI QÌ 機器

mask

MIÀN JÙ 面具

metal

JIN SHU
金屬

mirror

JÌNG ZI 鏡子

money

QIÁN 錢

mud

NÍ 泥

mug

BEI ZI 杯子

napkin

CAN JIN 餐巾

needle
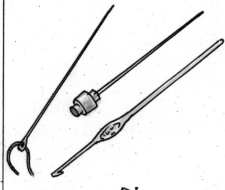
ZHEN 針

nest

KE 窠

net
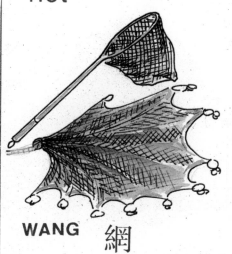
WANG 網

newspaper

BÀO 報

oil

YOÚ 油

paint

QÍ 漆

parcel

BAO GUO 包裹

pedal

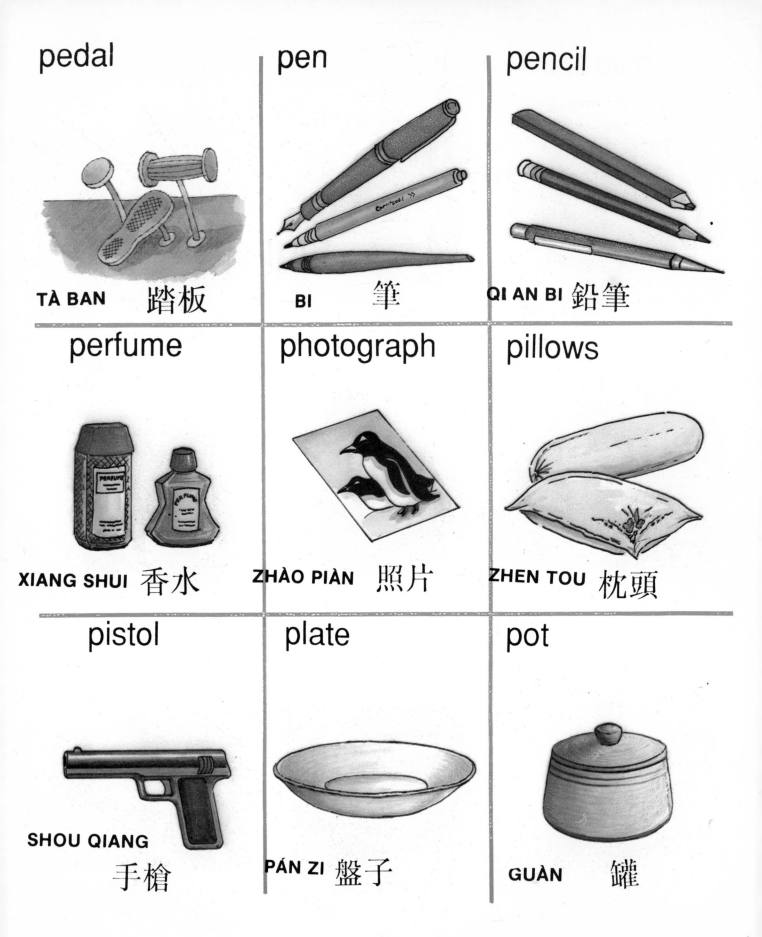

TÀ BAN 踏板

pen

BI 筆

pencil

QI AN BI 鉛筆

perfume

XIANG SHUI 香水

photograph

ZHÀO PIÀN 照片

pillows

ZHEN TOU 枕頭

pistol

SHOU QIANG

手槍

plate

PÁN ZI 盤子

pot

GUÀN 罐

118

powder

TALC POWDER

FEN 粉

pump

DA QÌ TONG

打氣筒

purse

QIÁN BAO

錢包

quilt

BÈI ZI 被子

razors

TÌ DAO 剃刀

refrigerator

BING XIANG

冰箱

register

DENG JÌ BEN 登記本

ribbon

DÀI ZI 帶子

robot

JI QÌ RÉN

機器人

rod
GÙN ZI 棍子

roll
JUAN 捲

rope
SHÉNG 繩

sack
DÀI ZI 袋子

saw
JÙ 鋸

scissors
JIAN DÀO 剪刀

screws
LUÒ SI DÌNG 螺絲釘

shadow
JING ZI 影子

shampoo
XI FÀ JÌ 洗髮劑

120

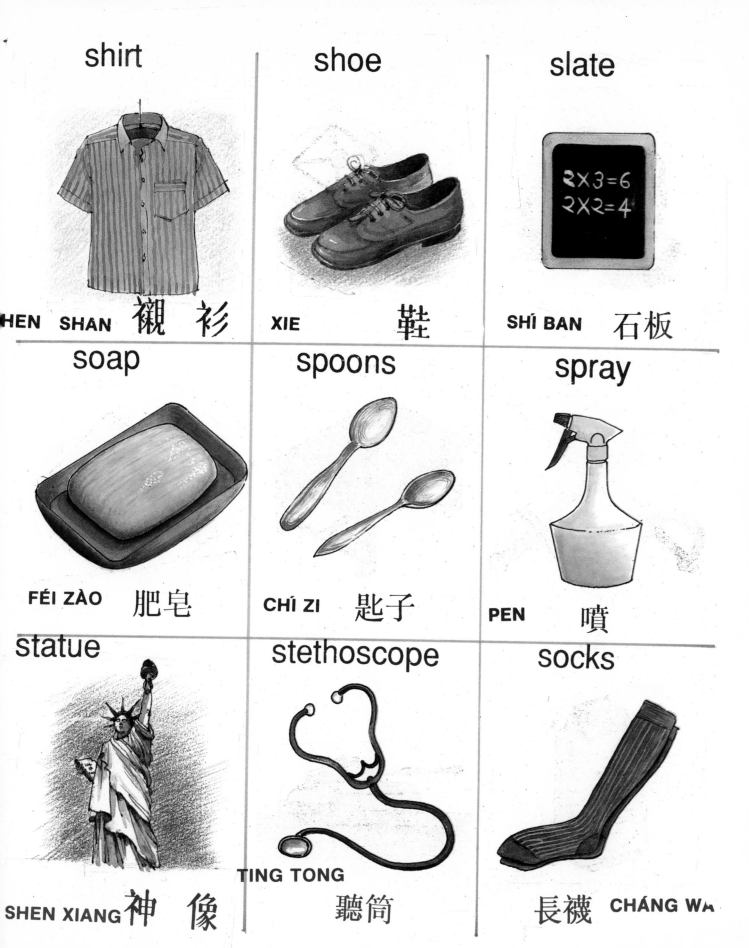

shirt

CHEN SHAN 襯衫

shoe

XIE 鞋

slate

SHÍ BAN 石板

soap

FÉI ZÀO 肥皂

spoons

CHÍ ZI 匙子

spray

PEN 噴

statue

SHEN XIANG 神像

stethoscope

TING TONG 聽筒

socks

長襪 CHÁNG WA

121

stone	stove	switches
SHÍ TOU 石頭	LÚ 爐	開關 KAI GUAN
sword	table	tag
JIÀN 劍	ZHUO ZI 桌子	BIAO QIAN 標簽
talcum powder	tank	thermometer
SHUANG SHEN FEN 爽身粉	TAN KÈ 坦克	WEN DÙ BIAO 溫度計

thread	ticket	timber
XIÀN 綫	**PIÀO** 票	**MÙ CÁI** 木材
tin	tools	towel
XI 錫	**GONG JÙ** 工具	**MÁO JIN** 毛巾
trap	tray	treasure
BU SHU QÌ 捕鼠器	**PÁN** 盤	**CÁI FÙ** 財富

tube

GUAN 管

type writer

打字機

umbrella

SAN 傘

utensils

QÌ MIN 器皿

vaseline

FÁN SHÌ LÍN 凡士林

vault

CÁI KÙ 財庫

video machine

錄相機 **LU XIANG JI**

wallet

PÍ JIA ZI 皮夾子

washing-machine

洗衣機 **XI YI JI**

watch

BIAO 表

water fall

PÙ BÙ 瀑布

weapon

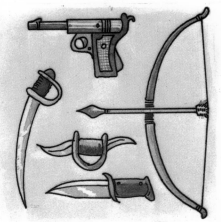

WU QÌ 武器

web

ZHI ZHU WANG

蜘蛛網

wing

CHÌ BANG 翅膀

whistle

SHÀO ZI 哨子

workshop

GONG CHANG 工場（场）

zip

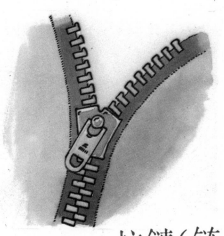

拉鏈（链）

LA LIÁN

INDEX

blue	54	canary	15
boat	96	candle	110
body	48	captain	62
bomb	109	car	96
bone	48	caravan	96
book	109	cards (playing)	110
bottles	109	carnation	83
bowl	40	carpenter	62
box	109	carpet	41
boy	61	carrom board	91
brain	48	carrots	29
branch	82	cart	97
bread	28	castle	71
brick	109	cat	15
bride	61	caterpillar	15
bridegroom	61	cathedral	71
bridge	70	cauliflower	29
brother	61	cave	71
brown	54	ceiling	41
brushes	109	centipede	15
bucket	41	cereal	29
buffalo	14	chain	110
bull	14	chair	41
bull fight	91	chandelier	41
bun	29	cheek	48
bungalow	70	cheese	29
bus	96	cheetah	15
bush	82	chef	62
bustard	15	cheque	110
butter	29	cherry	29
buttercup	82	chess	91
butterfly	15	chest	48
buttons	110	chicken	16
		child	62
cabbage	29	chillies	30
cabin	41	chimney	41
cabinet	41	chimpanzee	16
cable	110	chocolate	30
cactus	82	church	71
cafe	71	cinema	71
cage	110	circle	54
cake	29	circus	72
calf	15	city	71
camel	15	clarinet	91
camera	110	clinic	72
camp	71	cloth	42
canal	71	cloud	102

clown	62	dancers	62
coach	97	dandelion	83
coal	111	dates	30
coast	72	daughter	62
cobra	16	decimal	54
cock	16	deer	17
cockroach	16	den	72
coconut	30	dentist	63
coffee	30	desert	73
coins	111	desk	111
college	72	dew	103
comb	111	dinosaur	17
comet	102	dish	112
computer	111	doctor	63
conductor	62	dog	17
cone	54	dolphin	17
cook	62	dome	73
cooker	42	donkey	17
cord	111	door	42
corn	83	drain	42
corner	72	drawer	112
cornet	91	dressing table	42
cot	42	driver	63
cottage	72	drought	103
cotton	83	drugs	112
country	72	drum	91
court	72	duck	17
cow	16	dustbin	112
crab	16	dwarf	63
crane	97		
cricket	91	eagle	18
crocodile	16	ear	49
crow	16	earth quake	103
crowd	62	eclipse	103
cub	17	egg	30
cube	54	egg plant	83
cuckoo	17	eight	11
cucumber	30	elbow	49
cupboard	42	electrician	63
currants	30	elephant	18
curtain	42	elevator	42
cushion	111	elm	83
cylinder	111	engine	97
		envelope	112
daffodil	83	eraser	112
dagger	111	escalator	43
daisy	83	exhibition	73

eye	49	garage	74
		garage	43
face	49	garbage	13
facsimile	97	garden	74
factory	73	garden	43
falcon	18	garlic	31
family	63	gate	43
fans	112	generator	97
farm	73	geranium	84
farmer	63	gift	113
father	63	ginger	31
fence	43	giraffe	19
fern	83	girl	64
field	73	glacier	74
fig	30	glass	113
finger	49	glider	97
fir	84	globe	103
fire	112	glove	113
fire fighter	63	glue	113
fish	18	goat	18
fish	31	goblet	113
five	11	goggles	113
flag	112	golf	92
flamingo	18	goose	19
flax	84	gorilla	19
flood	103	grand child	64
flour	31	grand father	64
flower pot	43	grand mother	64
flute	91	grapefruit	31
fly	18	grapes	31
foam	43	grass	84
fog	103	green	54
foot	49	grocery	31
football	92	guitar	92
forehead	49	gulf	74
forest	73	gum	113
fork	43	guns	114
fort	73		
fountain	113	hair	49
four	11	hammer	114
fox	18	hand	49
frog	18	handkerchief	114
fruit	31	handle	114
fur	113	hare	19
furniture	43	hats	114
		head	50
gallery	73	heap	54

owl	22		plate	45
ox	22		platform	77
			play ground	77
paint	117		plumber	66
painter	66			
pair	56		plums	35
palace	76		polar bear	23
palm	51		policeman	66
palm tree	86		pond	77
pan	44		pony	23
panda	22		pool	77
panther	22		porcupine	23
papaya	34		port	77
parachute	98		porter	66
parcel	117		post card	98
park	77		postman	66
parrot	22		post office	77
parsley	86		pot	118
pavement	77		potatoes	34
peach	34		powder	119
peacock	22		pram	45
peanuts	34		priest	67
pear	34		prince	67
peas	87		prison	78
pedal	118		pudding	35
pelican	22		pump	119
pen	118		pumpkin	35
pencil	118		puppet	93
penguin	22		puppy	23
peony	87		purse	119
people	66			
peppers	34		quail	23
perfume	118		queen	67
petrol pump	98		quilt	119
photograph	118			
piano	93		rabbit	23
pickle	34		racket	93
pie	34		radio	98
pigeon	23		radish	35
pillar	77		raft	98
pillows	118		rain	104
pilot	66		rainbow	104
pineapple	34		raisins	35
pink	57		raspberry	35
pistol	118		rat	23
planet	104		razors	119
plate	118		rectangle	57
			red	57

redwood	87		shadow	120
refrigerator	119		shampoo	120
register	119		shamrock	87
reindeer	23		shark	24
restaurant	78		shed	78
rhinoceros	24		sheep	24
rib	51		shelf	45
ribbon	119		shephard	67
rice	35		ship	99
river	78		shirt	121
road	78		shoe	121
robber	67		shop	78
robot	119		shopkeeper	67
rod	120		shoulder	51
roll	120		shower	45
roof	45		shuttle cock	93
root	87		signal	99
rope	120		sink	45
rose	87		sisters	67
rug	45		sitar	93
			six	11
saccharin	35		skates	93
sack	120		skeleton	51
sage	87		ski	93
sailor	67		skin	52
saint	67		skull	52
salad	35		sky	105
salt	36		skyscraper	78
sandwich	36		slate	121
satellite	104		sledge	99
saturn	104		small	57
sauce	36		smoke	45
sausages	36		snacks	36
saw	120		snail	24
school	78		snake	24
scissors	120		snow	105
scooter	98		soap	121
scorpion	24		socks	121
screws	120		sofa	46
sea	105		solar system	105
seagull	24		soldier	68
sea horse	24		solicitor	68
seal	24		son	68
seat	45		soup	36
seesaw	93		soyabeans	36
seven	11		space	105
			spaghetti	36

sparrow	25	tank	122
sphere	57	tanker	99
spider	25	tap	46
spinach	36	taxi	99
spoons	121	tea	37
spray	121	teacher	68
spring	105	teeth	52
square	57	telephone	99
squirrel	25	television	99
stadium	79	telex	100
stage	79	temple	79
stamp	99	ten	11
stars	105	tennis	94
station	79	theatre	79
statue	121	thermometer	122
steps	46	thick	58
stethoscope	121	thief	68
stockings	121	thin	58
stomach	52	thorn	88
stone	122	thread	123
storm	105	three	11
stove	122	throat	52
strawberry	37	thumb	52
street	79	thunder	106
submarine	99	ticket	123
subway	79	tiger	25
sugar	37	timber	123
sugarcane	87	tin	123
summer	106	toad	25
sun	106	toast	37
sunflower	87	tobacco	88
super market	79	toffee	38
swan	25	toilet	46
sweet corn	37	tomato	38
sweet pototoes	37	ton	58
sweets	37	tongue	52
swimming pool	79	tools	123
swing	93	tooth brush	46
switches	122	tornado	106
sword	122	tortoise	25
syrup	37	towel	123
		tower	80
table	122	town	80
tag	122	toy	94
talcum (powder)	122	tractor	100
tall	57	train	100
tangerine	37	tram car	100

trap	123		wasp	26
tray	123		watch	125
treasore	123		water	38
tree	88		waterfall	125
triangle	58		waterlily	88
trumpet	94		watermelon	38
tub	46		weapon	125
tubes	124		web	125
tulip	88		whale	26
tunnel	80		wheat	38
turkey	25		wheel	100
turnip	38		whistle	125
turtle	25		white	58
two	11		wicket	94
type writer	124		wife	68
typhoon	106		window	46
			wing	125
umbrella	124		winter	106
university	80		wolf	26
utensils	124		woman	68
			woodpecker	26
valley	80		workshop	125
van	100		worm	26
vanilla	88		wrestlers	68
vaseline	124		wrist	52
vault	124			
vegetables	38		xylo phone	94
vehicle	100			
verandah	80		yacht	100
video machine	124		yak	26
village	80		yam	88
violet	58		yard	58
violet	88		yellow	58
violin	94		yoghurt	38
volcano	106			
volley ball	94		zebra	26
vulture	26		zero	11
			zinnias	88
wagon	100		zip	125
waist	52		zoo	80
waiter	68			
wall	46			
wallet	124			
walnut	38			
ward	80			
wardrobe	46			
washing machine	124			

□ □

INDEX : CHINESE WORDS
(Romanised)

CHINESE INDEX CONCLUDED